© Publication: Penguin Random House South Africa (Pty) Ltd,
The Estuaries No 4, Oxbow Crescent, Century Avenue, Century City 7441
PO Box 1144, Cape Town 8000
www.penguinrandomhouse.co.za

© Text: Disemelo Hoaeane, Monene Mathiba, Matodzi Amisi,
          Misokuhle Nyathikazi, Mpumi Mbethe, Nyasha Williams,
          Phuthanang Motsielwa, Shikombiso Kimeto,
          Shirmoney Rhode, Thulisile Bhuda

© Illustrations: Sanelisiwe Singaphi 2023
Publisher: Nandi Lessing-Venter

Cover typography and layout by Renthia Buitendag — Stickart
Set in 18 pt on 22 pt Futura Book

Printed by ABC Press

First edition 2023

ISBN 978 0 637 00145 8 (Print)
ISBN 978 0 637 00146 5 (Ebook)

THE SOUTH AFRICAN ALPHABET OF AFFIRMATIONS

ILLUSTRATED BY SANELISIWE SINGAPHI

WRITTEN BY
- **DISEMELO HOAEANE**
- **MONENE MATHIBA**
- **MATODZI AMISI**
- **MISOKUHLE NYATHIKAZI**
- **MPUMI MBETHE**
- **NYASHA WILLIAMS**
- **PHUTHANANG MOTSIELWA**
- **SHIKOMBISO KIMETO**
- **SHIRMONEY RHODE**
- **THULISILE BHUDA**

Penguin
Random House
South Africa

www.penguinrandomhouse.co.za

Aa

Amba
Speak

Language: TshiVenda

Ndi a ḓi ambela, ipfi ḽanga ndi ḽanga. Zwine nda amba ndi zwine nda ita.

I will speak for myself. I own my voice. I will honour my words.

4

Bb
Boemanokeng
Support

Language: Setswana

Botshelo bo nkema nokeng
ka dinako tsotlhe.
Kitso ya me ya tlholego e
ntshegetsa ka dinako tsotlhe.

As I walk through life,
there is always support
available to me. My
intuition (inner knowing)
supports me at all times.

Cc

Language: XiTsonga

Chivirika
Zealous

Impassioned, fiery, fired-up, passionate

Ndzi chivirikela vutomi bya mina hi ku tiyimisela. A ndzi pfumeleri munhu hambi ku ri mani a tima ku hiseka loku ku nga kona embilwini ya mina.

I am passionate about my life. I don't let anyone put out the fire in me.

Dd
Dala

Language: isiZulu

I am created

Continually evolving masterpiece

Ngidalwe ngendlela ehlukile futhi ngiyazi qhenya ngami. Ngiwum'sebenzi wobuciko.

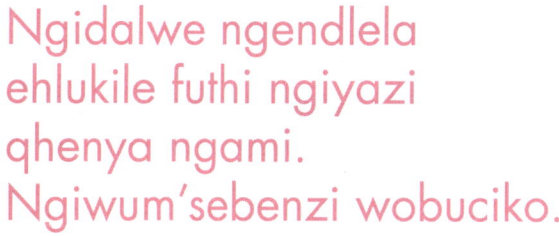

I am created differently and I'm proud of who I am. I am a work of art.

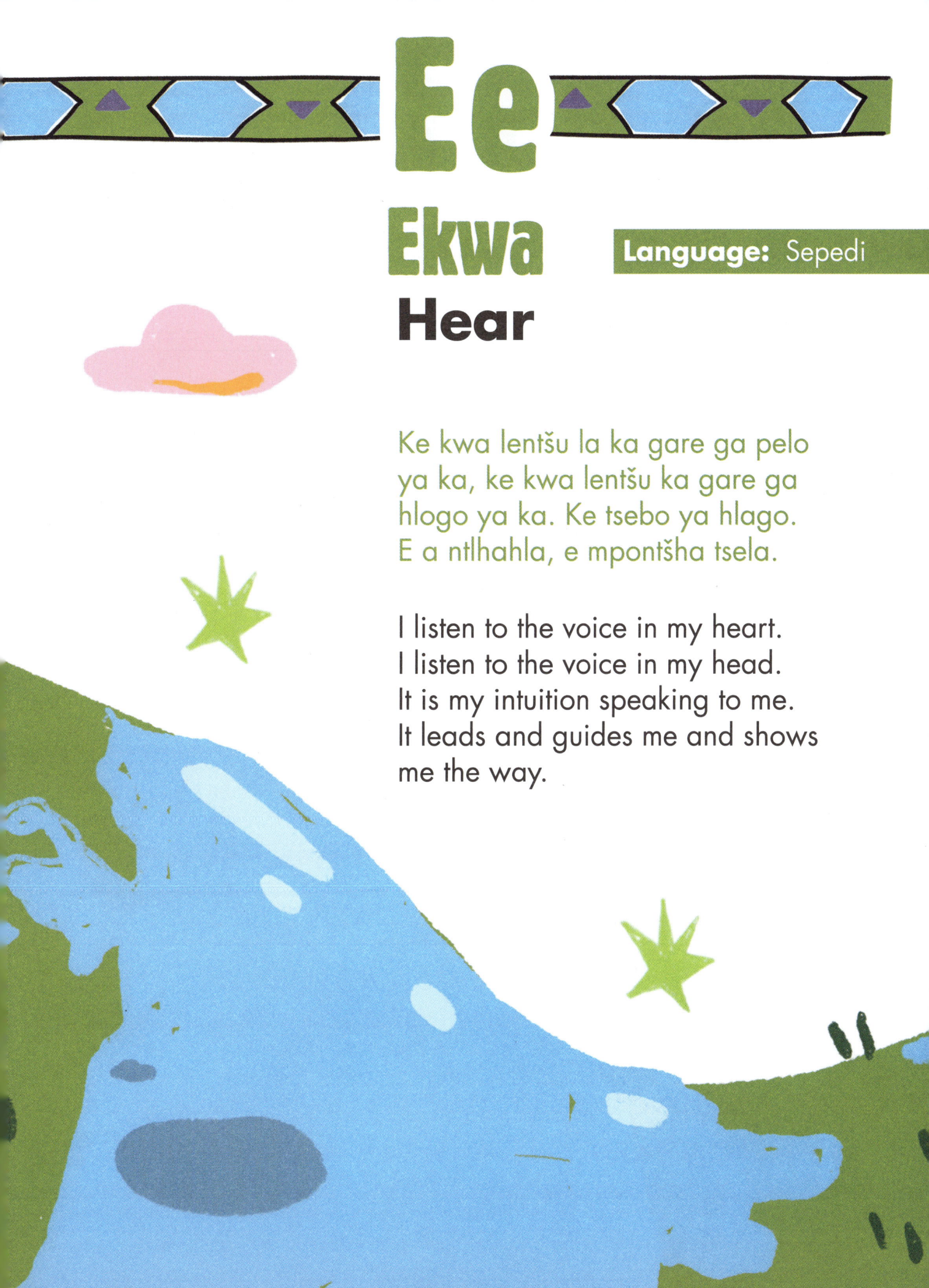

Ee

Ekwa
Hear

Language: Sepedi

Ke kwa lentšu la ka gare ga pelo
ya ka, ke kwa lentšu ka gare ga
hlogo ya ka. Ke tsebo ya hlago.
E a ntlhahla, e mpontšha tsela.

I listen to the voice in my heart.
I listen to the voice in my head.
It is my intuition speaking to me.
It leads and guides me and shows
me the way.

F f

Fofa
Fly

Language: Sesotho

Let go of limitations, take a chance

Ke tla ithuta ho fofa jwalo ka nonyana, ke tsebe ho bona lefatshe, ke hodise tsebo ea ka.

I'll teach myself to fly like a bird so that I can see the world and grow my knowledge.

Gg

Language: isiSwati

Gidza
Traditional dance

KuGidza kuhlahlambisa kuphindze kuvocavoce umtimba wami, loku kuyangitfokotisa emoyeni wami, inhlitiyo yami iyajabula.

Dancing improves and exercises my body. When I am feeling sad, dancing makes my heart and spirit happy again.

Hh
Hlaziya
Refresh

Language: isiXhosa

Ndiyakwazi ukuhlaziya ingqondo yam, kunye nomzimba wam, endicinga ngalo, n okuthola ulwazi nokucela uncedo xa ndiludinga.

I am self-aware and able to review my thoughts and communicate my needs so that I grow continuously. I refresh my thoughts, my body, and ways of doing things. My growth comes from gaining knowledge and asking for help when I need it.

Ii

Ithuba
Chance
Opportunity

Language: isiNdebele

Nginekghono lokufeza koke engikufaka emkhumbulweni wami. Kufanele ngizinikeze ithuba lelo.

I am able to fulfill everything I set my mind on. I welcome an opportunity that is for my highest good.

Jj
Jollie
Happy

Language: Afrikaans

Ek is jollie en lag hard uit my maag. Ek begin my dag met vreugde en dankbaarheid. Ek voel goed en groei elke keer as ek vrolik is.

I am happy and laugh loudly from my belly. I start my day with joy and gratitude. I heal and grow each time I jump with glee.

15

K k

Khetha
Choose

Language: isiZulu

Ngikhetha injabulo yami.
Ngikhetha ik'sasa lami.
Ngikhetha ukuthula kanye nothando.

I choose my happiness.
I choose my future.
I choose peace and love.

L l

Londola

Language: TshiVenda

Care
Diligent

Ndi a ḓi londa, ndi ḓi fara zwavhuḓi, ndi londola hune nda dzula hone, ngauri ri na shango ḽithihi fhedzi, hayani hashu.

I take care of myself, I hold my head high. I also take care of my surroundings because we have only one earth, our home.

Mm
Mukela

Language: isiSwati

Accept
Embrace
Welcome

Ngiyatitsandza, ngitsandza yonkhe intfo ngami. Ngemukela wonkhe muntfu nebuntfu bakhe, ngetandla letifutfumele, ngaphandle kwekucwaya bantfu.

I love myself and accept all of myself unconditionally with grace and compassion. I accept all people for who they are with a warm embrace.

N n
Ndlela
Path

Language: XiTsonga

Ntila wa mina wa vutomi wu woxe, wu hambanile ni mintila ya van'wana. Milorho ya mina yi tshamisekile. Vumundzuku bya mina ndzi ta byi yimela. Ndzi tsakela rendzo leri ndzi nga e ka rona.

My path in life is unique. My dreams are valid. I defend my tomorrow. I love the journey I am on.

Oo

Opela
Sing

Language: Sepedi

Ke ikopantšha le setšhaba sa gešo ge ke opela. Ke bontšha maikutlwo a ka ge ke opela.

I am united with my tribe, communities, and nation as I lift my voice. I express my emotions and feelings as I sing.

Pp
Peo
Seed

Language: Sesotho

Ke peo ya lefatshe, kenna khoro ea bophelo. Ke motheo oo ereng ha o hlokometswe, ke ate ho ba menyetla e sa feleng.

I am a seed. I am a gateway to life. I am the foundation that when nurtured, I will grow into endless possibilities.

Qq
Qiqa
Think deeply

Language: isiXhosa

Ndisebenzisa ingqiqo kunye nethuku ukwenza isigqibo esinolwazi. Ndiyaziqonda iimpazamo ziyenzeka kwaye ndikhetha ukufunda kuzo.

I use logic and my intuition to make informed decisions. I understand mistakes can happen and I choose to learn from them.

Rr
Roroma

Language: Setswana

Abundance of all

Lefatshe le a roroma, Ke bontletsetletse ba dikotla le tshiamo. Tsotlhe ke tsa me le rona rotlhe go iketla ka tsone. Ke tshela ka ditebogo.

The world vibrates with abundance, nourishment, and wellness. There is enough for me and everyone. I live in thanks.

Ss

Stêk
Strong

Language: Afrikaans (Kaaps)

Ek is stêk, in my gedagtes, liggaam en gees. Ek erken as ekkie stêk voelie, en draai na annes toe vi' onnesteuning.

I am strong, in mind, body, and spirit. I admit when I don't feel strong and turn to others for support.

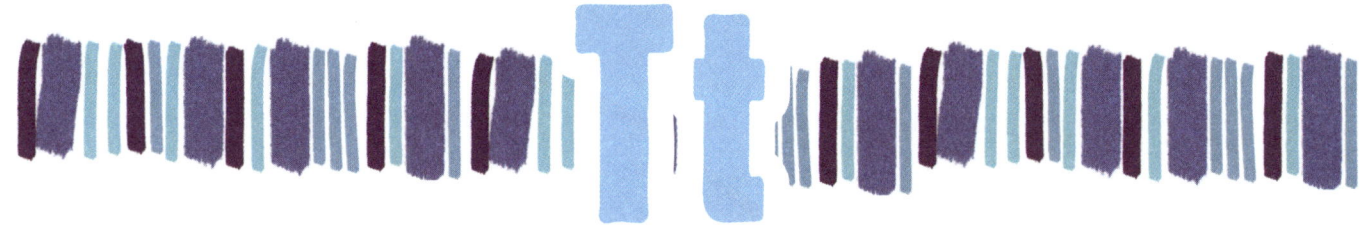

Tt

Thuso
Help

Language: TshiVenda

Ndi a humbela thuso ndi tshi i ṱoda. U humbela thuso ndi u vha wa nungo. Ndi thusa vhaṅwe vha tshi ṱoda thuso.

I do not have to do it all myself. I am brave enough to ask for help. And helping others makes them achieve their potential.

Uu

Ukuzithemba

Language: isiNdebele

Confidence
Believing in yourself

Ukuzithemba kwami kwenza ngisebenzele emabhudangwenami begodu ngibone nawowoke amakghono enginawo. Nginomoya wokukatelela begodu ngizinikele ngokupheleleko ekulemukeni woke amakghono enginawo.

My belief in myself enables me to work on my dreams and experience my full potential. I have a spirit of resilience and a strong will to explore all my talents.

Vv

Vela/Veta

Show up
Show

Language: isiSwati

Ngiya Vela nami eveni angisabi kuVeta lukhono lwami.

I show up in the world. I am not afraid to showcase my talent.

Ww

Wetsa
Digest

Language: Setswana

Ke wetsa dijo tse di monate tse ke di jang. Mmele wa me o bona matla go re ke kgone botshelo.

I digest the delicious food that I eat. My body receives the energy it needs to get through each day.

Xx

Xonga (ku xonga)

Gorgeous
Beautiful

Ndzi xongile. Na swona ndzi pfumelela ku xonga ka mina ka le ndzeni ku hatima e matihlweni ya mina ku voniwa hi mani na mani. Ndzi hanya ndzi ri karhi ndzi xiyaxiya ku saseka ka swilo hinkwanso.

I am beautiful. I let my inner beauty exude through my eyes for everyone to see it. I live each day to notice the beauty that is all around me.

Y y

Language: isiXhosa

Yomelela
Have strength

Ndiyakwazi ukuzomeleza xa ndijongene nengxaki zobomi, kwimihla ngemihla. Ndiyajongana nezinto ezoyikisayo ngothando nesibindi.

I have inner strength and each day I am able to persevere through situations and challenges. I face my fears with love and courage.

Z z

iZwe
Nation

Language: isiZulu

Ngiyi ngane yalesizwe.
Ngiyi mpumelelo
yokhokho bami.
Ngingum'Afrika.

I am a child of this
nation. I am my
ancestors' successes.
I am African.

About the
Authors

DISEMELO HOAEANE

Disemelo Hoaeane is an adventurous lady who is inspired by exploring nature and eager to have new experiences. She and her family are based in Johannesburg, South Africa. However, she is a strong believer that we should not be bound by geographical boundaries. She is a professional who creates online solutions focused on ensuring great user experience and interactions. Having children has ignited her passion to teach children about the history of their existence in order to craft a meaningful future ahead.

MATODZI AMISI

Matodzi Amisi is a mother of two and a research/ evaluation consultant with a keen interest in M&E and evidence use in the violence prevention sector, focusing on what works to prevent violence against women and children. She has been involved in several research projects including mapping of evidence on interventions to prevent violence in South Africa. Since 2016 she has been involved in the Violence Prevention Forum to promote collaboration between government, academia, and civil society in the generation of evidence of what works to prevent violence against children. She is a published author, having participated in two chapter books and several academic papers.

MONENE MATHIBA

Monene Mathiba lives in Pretoria, South Africa, with her two sons and husband. She is a finance and a public health specialist. She loves photography and all things creative. During her downtime, she enjoys reading, being one with nature and spending time with family. Traveling and discovering new places occupy a big space in her heart. She loves children and believes in the importance of assuring children with grounding words of affirmation.

MISOKUHLE NYATHIKAZI

Misokuhle Nyathikazi is a professional chef born and bred on the north side of the Amajuba mountains in a town called Newcastle (KwaZulu-Natal). She was raised by a teacher and was taught about the importance of education from a young age. She has lived and worked all over South Africa, which has given her the opportunity to indulge in the country's beauty and experience the different cultures along with their cuisines. She has also worked in the United States of America where she was introduced to (and ultimately fell in love with) West Indian food and culture. She is passionate about food and travel and plans to explore the world as much as she possibly can.

MPUMI MBETHE

Mpumi Mbethe holds a BA degree in journalism from the University of Johannesburg where she majored in communications and sociology. She began her broadcasting career as a production assistant on The Big Debate. She worked for Multichoice's Electronic Content Division, before trying out TV presenting on SABC youth programmes such as Ses'khona, ZONED and IDENTITY. In 2014 she joined SABC's siSwati radio station, where she co-hosted the afternoon drive show. It was in the same year that she summited the highest point in Africa, Mount Kilimanjaro, with the Trek4Mandela team lead by world record-holding mountaineer Sibusiso Vilane (the first black African to summit Mount Everest). In 2015 she joined the breakfast show on Ligwalagwala FM. She is currently the host of Mid Mornings on RISEfm. When she is not doing radio, she's a part-time social science researcher – facilitating focus groups or doing data analysis for qualitative studies for policy development in different sectors. She's an avid book reader and the chairperson of the executive board of Childline Mpumalanga. As a mother, she actively seeks content that is inclusive and representative for her children to consume a different, more empowering narrative of African people.

NYASHA WILLIAMS

Nyasha Williams is the author of the best-selling *I Affirm Me*, plus *Black Tarot / Ancestral Illumination, Keep Dreaming, Black Child, I Am Somebody, Ally Baby Can*, and *Alchemist Elements Oracle Deck, Guidebook and Guided Journal.*

SHIKOMBISO KIMETO

Shikombiso Kimeto is a Pretoria-based wife and mother of two – a girl and a boy. She is passionate about the journey of parenting. Being a professional in the learning space, she views learning as a gift and finds meaning in seeing the transformative power of self-discovery. Her views about life are strongly grounded by her upbringing in the north of South Africa and influenced by her experiences in Kenya, East Africa. She's learning to see the world through many lenses. She loves to travel, trying out new cooking recipes, creating beauty in living spaces, and tapping along to the sound of good music. She believes in creating a safe space for her children to thrive and fail forward.

PHUTHANANG MOTSIELWA

Phuthanang Motsielwa lives in South Africa with her husband and two children, a boy and a girl, whom she homeschools. She also enjoys corporate governance through serving as a board member of various entities. Phuthanang is passionate about life, nature, early childhood development, wealth creation, the human body, and travel.

SHIRMONEY RHODE

Shirmoney Rhode is an Afrikaans teacher, author, and performance poet hailing from Elsies River on the Cape Flats. She predominantly writes in Kaapse Afrikaans and is committed to telling (and retelling) stories of marginalized and dispossessed people of colour. Her debut collection, *Nomme 20 Delphistraat*, was published in 2016 and she's currently working on her second collection. She holds a BA (Hons) in Afrikaans from the University of the Western Cape and currently teaches at Claremont High School.

THULISILE BHUDA

Thulisile Bhuda is a culture activist, an indigenous scholar, and a lecturer at the University of Mpumalanga. She holds a MA degree in indigenous knowledge systems from the North-West University, and is currently busy with her PhD. Thulisile Bhuda specialises in isiNdebele ethnomathematics and African cultural expressions. Her work on isiNdebele ethnomathematics focuses on mathematical ideas and concepts used/found in amaNdebele beaded attires and mural art. Thulisile Bhuda believes that amaNdebele women are ethnoma-thematicians who rarely attended formal school yet understand symmetrical geometry. She has been featured on numerous media platforms such as TV, radio, magazines, and newspapers based on her interests as an indigenous scholar of indigenous knowledge systems. Her interests include decolonization of education, indigenous knowledge preservation, protection, management, and dissemination.